Stay Positive

By Cole Ryan

Table of Contents

A special thanks to Randy and Veronica Johnson.

Week 1

"In the beginning, God created the heaven and the earth. And the earth was without form, and void; and darkness was upon the face of the deep. And the Spirit of God moved upon the face of the waters. And God said, Let there be light: and there was light. And God saw the light, that it was good, and God divided the light from the darkness." ~ Genesis 1:1-4

Let's start this year off with a bang!

Did you know that, when Jesus speaks, darkness flees (Genesis 1)? When He steps onto the scene, demons tremble (Matthew 8), and we have no choice but to bow (John 18)? If God can do all these things, why does He want us? Because He's an artist, the greatest artist, and we are His workmanship. *Me?* Yes, you, "Before I formed you in the womb I knew you before you were born; I set you apart; I appointed you as a prophet to the nations." (Jeremiah 1:5)

Now, don't let this go to your head, though we still should humble ourselves in His presence, *which is effectively everywhere. But surely not I?* some of you might be thinking. *Do you know who am I and what I've done?* Me, no. But God does, and He doesn't care. He calls who He calls, and if He calls you, who are you to say no? He doesn't call the qualified, He qualifies the called, and if He's qualified you, then no man, angel, demon, devil, nor government can stop you.

Have a blessed week.

Week 2

"For God so loved the world, that He gave His only begotten Son, that whosoever believeth in Him should not perish, but have everlasting life." ~ John 3:16

Let's start with a story. There was a man whose wife died. The man loved his wife very much and lamented greatly at the news of her death, but there was a small light at the end of the tunnel, a son, his only link to his deceased spouse.

One day in the country that he lived in, there was an outbreak with a new virus. The doctors were dumbfounded not only by how fast it was spreading, but also how fast it was killing people, so in an attempt to keep the people safe, the doctors suggested for the people to get tested and stay at home, and the people complied. The man responded to the call and got his son and himself tested.

A few days pass, and he receives a letter in the mail from the hospital, asking for him to return. Worried, the man wastes no time taking his son and immediately returning to the hospital.

Once there, he sits down with the doctor, while his son plays in the corner. The doctor tells the man that, while doing some blood work on the sample of blood he gave them, that they found a cure. The man smiles. *That's good news*, he thinks, but the doctor has a disturbed look on his face.

"Yes, we found a cure to beat this virus, but to make it would more than likely kill the host."

The man looks at his son, and then back to the doctor. "If it means I can keep my son safe, I'll do it."

The doctor grits his teeth. "I'm sorry to tell you this, sir, I am, but it wasn't your blood that contains the cure."

How many parents would willingly give up their children's lives to save humanity? I would assume not many, if any at all, yet God did.

Let's take a look at the virus that was plaguing this country and replace it with something that operates similarly—sin. Sin spreads fast and kills just as quickly, if not faster, than any virus. Yet, despite this "virus," God gave up his only son for people like you and me. Let's keep this in mind as we go about our week.

Have a blessed week.

Week 3

"For I know the thoughts that I think toward you, saith the Lord, thoughts of peace, and not of evil, to give you an expected end." ~ Jeremiah 29:11

This is one of, if not my favorite, verses from the Bible. Though there are many verses in scripture that key you into God's character, in my opinion, there's just something about this verse that someone can't help but be at peace with, knowing that God's intentions for us are not for our calamity but our success.

In the book of Luke, it says, "Which of you fathers, if your son asks for a fish, will give him a snake instead? ... If you then, being evil, know how to give good gifts to your children, how much more will your heavenly Father give the Holy Spirit to those who ask Him?"

God wants what's best for us; there's no doubt in my mind about that. But it's not just going to happen. We have to want it for ourselves. Will it be easy? Not always, but rest assured that our Heavenly Father is for us and not against us, and is an ever-present help in dark times.

Will you trust Him enough to be in your corner?

Have a blessed week.

Week 4

"...However, the body is not for sexual immorality but for the Lord, and the Lord for the body." ~ 1 Corinthians 6:13

It's not easy to stay away from sexual immorality. If I can be blunt, between thoughts betraying you and nowadays due to how easy it is to access adult sites, toys, and whatever else, one can say it's borderline impossible to resist temptation in that area. Thankfully, we serve a God who has a Doctorate in taking impossible situations and making the possible for our benefit. "And we know that all things work together for good to them that love God, to them who are the called according to his purpose." (Romans 8:28)

Lust of the eyes and flesh is nothing new. It's been around since Biblical times, and no one was above its temptation. Adam and Eve (Lust of the eyes), David and Bathsheba (Lust of the flesh), even Jesus was tempted with these things, including the pride of life. (Matthew 4:1-11)

Now, do I think you're going to be able to play everything off as Jesus did? No, I don't. But one thing I do know is, if you resist temptation, it will flee from you. There will be times when we fail at resisting, but remember, even though we fall, we can still get back up again.

"For a just man falls seven times, and rises up again..." ~ Proverbs 24:16

Have a blessed week.

Week 5

"I have said these things to you, that in Me you may have peace. In the world you will have tribulation. But take heart; I have overcome the world." ~ *John 16:33*

Have you ever been frustrated because you feel like you're being pulled five thousand different ways and struggling to keep it together? If you haven't, then you're better than most people. That's why it's so important to keep God in the forefront of your life, because life has turbulent moments that will shake you, moments that make you want to quit, moments that will make you feel trapped and call out for help.

Who or what are you clinging to when those moments come? Drugs? Porn? Alcohol? Those won't fix anything. That's like putting a Band-Aid on when you're diagnosed with cancer. It's not helping you in the slightest.

At the risk of sounding too preachy, but it's the truth, only Jesus can heal the sinking pit in your heart, and when you fall apart, he's the one who can pick up those pieces and put you back together again, stronger than attempting it on your own if you have faith in him and give him the chance to do so. Jesus is close to the broken-hearted and saves those who are crushed in spirit, but you have to be the one to make the choice to invite him in.

Have a blessed week.

Week 6

"Answer me quickly, LORD; my spirit fails. Don't hide Your face from me, or I will be like those going down to the Pit." ~ Psalm 143:7

Have you ever stopped and thought, *I feel so (swear word) overwhelmed right now; Jesus, where are you right now, why are you allowing this to happen to me, and what did I do to deserve this?"* Ask yourself, leading up to this event, did you by chance do anything to cause this situation based on your actions (i.e. Not going to work one day and coming in the next and you're just flooded with not only yesterday's work, but now you have to deal with today's as well)? But maybe you didn't do anything wrong, and it's just the situation you're in. If that's the case, the Lord's words of advice is: "Endure the Resistance."

Doing this isn't easy, but take heart in knowing your Savior is with you every step of the way. You will not fall, and though you might be going through the fire and the flames, you'll be coming out on the other side unbroken! Amen.

Prayer:

My prayer for you this week is that you take heart and know that God is for you and not against you. That you know He loves you, not in a manly kind of way, but an agape Godly type of love, and know He'll never leave you, even in the moments when it feels like He isn't there. As for the situation you're going through, whatever it may be, remember this: no weapon formed against you will prosper and *every* tongue that raises against you in judgment, the Lord will condemn.

Have a blessed week.

Week 7

"Since they were not able to bring him to Jesus because of the crowd, they removed the roof above him, and after digging through it, they lowered the mat on which the paralytic was lying." ~ Mark 2:4

Working in retail, you learn quickly that you have to think on the fly ... *a lot*, especially when things don't go according to plan.

Those four men in the book of Mark could have just given up and gone home when they couldn't get to Jesus, but if they had done that, we would have missed out on a tremendous act of faith. A type of faith that drove them to persevere. A type of faith that says, "I can't save you, but I know someone who can, and we're going to get you to him, come hell or high water."

The Bible didn't even give these men names, yet they are mentioned. Jesus even healed the man, but not because of anything the man did, but because of the faith those four men who lowered the man down had. Wouldn't it be amazing if we tackled our problems like that? Just imagine whatever insurmountable obstacle we face in our lives we "improvise" by digging a hole in the roof. You might have to work for it, but who knows? Faith just may pay off.

Have a blessed week.

Week 8

"What a person desires is unfailing love; better to be poor than a liar." ~ Proverbs 19:22

What does intimacy look and feel like? Not by man's standards, but how it was originally designed by God. The word "intimacy" means close familiarity or friendship; closeness.

It's funny yet understandable how we tend to mistake that word to mean sex. To be fair, sex is a part of intimacy, but only a part, because you can have sex with someone, go your separate ways, and not feel anything toward that person. Which is sad.

So, what more is there to intimacy other than sex? The Greeks have a word (probably more than one word, but humor me), Ginosko, which means *to personally, intimately, and experientially know something.* In this context, to say you want to be intimate with someone what you're actually saying is you want to know them on a deeper level. Not just on a physical level, but an emotional and spiritual level.

In the book of John, Jesus says that He knows His sheep and His sheep know him. That should tell us that he wants an intimate relationship with us. The questions are: do we want one with Him and what are we willing to sacrifice to be intimate with Him?

Have a blessed week.

Week 9

"'Knowing their thoughts,' Jesus said, 'Why do you entertain evil thoughts in your hearts?'" ~ Matthew 9:4

Why do we occupy our minds with thoughts that tell us things like: we'll never change, it'll always be this way, you can't do it so just give up, or you're not enough? We all have moments of self-doubt, and no one is exempt from them, and if you don't either A) you're in denial, or B) we need to invent a new word for the level of ego you're having (leaning towards self-conceit-egoism). Anyway, truth is, yeah, doubts and those thoughts will come, and you're not enough ... at least not on your own.

How we start our day can play a factor in how our day will play out. If you humor me for a few days, I think this can help. On your way to work or school or wherever, daily try quoting these scriptures every morning before you leave:

"This *is* the day the Lord has made; We will rejoice and be glad in it." (Psalm 118:24)

"No weapon formed against me will prosper and every tongue that raises against me in judgment, He shall condemn." (Isaiah 54:17)

"For the Spirit God gave us does not make us timid, but gives us power, love, and self-discipline." (2 Timothy 1:7)

These are just some words of empowerment I have been raised on and have stood the test of time in my life. Maybe they can help you in those times, as well.

Have a blessed week.

Week 10

"Where can I go from your Spirit? Where can I flee from your presence?" ~ *Psalms 139:7*

Do you ever feel like God is mad at you? Before I understood what it meant to be a follower of Christ, I did. The truth is He isn't mad at you, and when life enters the mix, it's easy to lose sight of that. Even when He feels far away, He's right there with you, in the hard times just as He's with you when things are going smoothly. There's no hiding from the presence of The Lord God Almighty, there's nowhere to run where He can't find you.

Now, to a nonbeliever, that will sound either scary or silly, but for a true follower of Christ, there's a comfort to be had. Why? Because you know that He cares for you.

"Which of you, if your son asks for bread, will give him a stone?" (Matthew 7:9)

Need more?

"Look at the birds of the air, for they neither sow nor reap nor gather into barns; yet your Heavenly Father feeds them. Are you not of more value than they?" (Matthew 6:26)

What I'm trying to say is God's not mad at you; He's madly in love with you. His mercy renews every day. He's the same yesterday, today, and forever. You're more than just a number to Him.

I'm not saying these things because I have nothing else better to say. I'm saying this to tell you that you're not alone. God's here. He has been this whole time. Stop listening to that devil telling you you're alone and no one's coming for you. HE ALREADY CAME! He's here! His name is Jesus Christ of Nazareth, and He loves you.

Have a blessed week.

Week 11

"Casting all your anxieties on Him, because He cares for you." ~ 1 Peter 5:7

As a non- or new believer, to hear something like *"casting your anxieties on Him because He cares for you,"* probably sounds crazy. "What? Am I just supposed to cast my worries to this invisible force and magically all my problems will vanish?" For one in that position, I can't blame you, I've known believers who struggle with that, as well. But, through determination (to seek His face), faith, and prayer, some of them learned there's truth in this scripture.

One thing I know without a shadow of a doubt is that God loves and cares for you. He doesn't enjoy watching us struggle. What kind of father delights watching His child suffer?

Not saying He can't use that pain, because He can use our hardships and suffering to draw us closer to Him. And that's all He wants. Forget the pulpit and the theatrics of some of the churches. Don't mistake me; it has its purpose. But at the end of the day, it's you who He wants. He wants that deep, intimate relationship with you, no hidden agendas, no nefarious schemes, not your money, just you.

Have a blessed week.

Week 12

"Count it all joy, my brothers, when you meet trials of various kinds, for you know that the testing of your faith produces steadfastness. And let steadfastness have its full effect, that you may be perfect and complete, lacking in nothing." ~ James 1:2-4

It might be controversial to say, but that boss or co-worker who leaves you wanting to tell Jesus to "Hold my drink" might not be all that bad. Nothing in this life happens by chance everything has a purpose. Whether for good or bad. Everything is for the glory of God, according to His purpose. Pressure makes diamonds.

What if I told you this season, you're in ... whatever it is that causes you sorrow and/or grief is building your endurance? Let me explain, I worked retail—*gasp*, I know, horrifying—and if you've worked retail, you might know where I'm going with this. Let me tell you, between ungrateful people and management nipping at your heels for an impossible deadline that leaves you looking at them like they've lost their mind, nothing humbles you quicker than working in retail. Looking back on it, however, I'm better for it. I'm a lot more temperate now because of it. I've learned when to speak my mind and when to keep it to myself. I've learned the world is full of ... not so nice people and not everyone has my best interest in mind. I'm not telling you this to boast; I'm telling you this to belabor a point. Though trials and tribulations may wear and tear you, but by the grace of God, they will not break and destroy you.

Have a blessed week.

Week 13

"I praise you, for I am fearfully and wonderfully made. Wonderful are your works; my soul knows it very well." ~ Psalm 139:14

One thing you have to give King David credit for is he knew how to worship his God. He worshiped Him when times were good, managed to praise Him when times were bad (Psalms 34), and he even praised the Lord when it led to him looking like a fool (2 Samuel 6). Don't we have a reason to praise the Lord just as he did? Did you not wake up today? Do you not have clothes on your back and a roof over your head? Do you not have health? The only kind of person who can't praise the Lord is a dead one (I mean that in a spiritual, as well as a literal, way).

And why shouldn't we praise the Lord? Don't you know your Maker knew you before you were born?

In the book of Jeremiah, it says, "Before I formed you in the womb, I knew you; before you were born, I set you apart; I appointed you as a prophet to the nations." He created you and me for a time such as this, and we're all different.

I once heard a Pastor named Keion Henderson say, "If you can do what I can do, and if I could do what you could do, then one of us is irrelevant."

God's works are incredible. Did you know your heart beats 70 times per minute and pumps about 2,000 gallons—7,500 liters—of blood per day? An average body contains nearly 100 trillion cells. The brain contains 100 billion nerve cells. Human kidneys process daily about 130 quarts—about 123 liters—of blood to filter out waste and water. Our skeletal system has 206 bones connected to an intricate system of tendons, cartilage, and ligaments. The skeletal system not only enables us to move but also helps to produce blood, and it stores calcium. I think science has its place, but when I see and read things like that I have to believe there's a God because there are some things in this world that are too detailed to be chalked up to chance, and you're one of those things.

Have a blessed week.

Week 14

"This is the day the Lord has made; let us rejoice and be glad in it." ~ Psalms 118:24

Why is it that sometimes we give people power over us that they don't deserve? Did they wake you up this morning? Was it them who blessed you with health and people who care about you?

Stop allowing people to dictate your feelings! Don't let people's foolishness distract you from praising the Lord your God. If you hold your peace and let the Lord fight your battle, victory shall be yours. Is it easy to give the Lord praise when storms come? No, but in the end, it'll be worth it because the Lord our God makes all things work together for our good according to His purpose. (Romans 8:28) And when you look back and see how God did so, and see the struggle, and see how God was with you every step of the way, and delivered you from your hardship, you won't be able not to worship and give Him praise.

Have a blessed week.

Week 15

"Jesus answered, 'I am the way and the truth and the life. No one comes to the Father except through me.'" ~ John 14:6

Lord God Almighty (El Shaddai), Shepard (Jehovah-Raah), Healer (Jehovah Rapha) are just a few of the names God goes by.

Did you know that there are many names to the God we worship? Well, if you didn't ... *surprise!* He does and rest assured they all identify the same Heavenly Father. Isn't that reassuring? That no matter what you might be going through God has a solution for your issue. That there's no area in your life that He doesn't know about, no area that He doesn't care about. He cares about you. Which is great. Isn't that why Jesus died? Was it not so we could have a more personal relationship with the Heavenly Father?

As we go through this week, let's focus on God's nature and reflect on the battles He's brought us through.

Have a blessed week.

Week 16

"And whosoever shall not receive you, nor hears your words, when ye depart out of that house or city, shake off the dust of your feet." ~ Matthew 10:14

How many times in your life have you been rejected or dejected for speaking the truth or just opening your heart and soul to someone? If you're honest with yourself, you could probably think of several times. Okay, Susie Q or Bobby J turned down your advances and it hurt like nobody's business, and at that moment, you probably wanted the earth to split apart and swallow you whole. What if I told you that the pain you felt in that moment doesn't have to weigh you down, and God can use that suffering as fuel for tomorrow's testimony, because what if that was no good for you in the first place (i.e. that person was only going to use you for or to get something)? Perhaps God saw what those people were saying behind your back and delivered you. Maybe He has someone better lined up for you, and if He doesn't, that's okay; use that energy elsewhere.

Paul said (as a concession), "I wish that all of you were as I am (Single). But each of you has your own gift from God; one has this gift, another has that." (1 Corinthians 7:7)

Some of you weren't meant to be married and, as painful as it may be to hear, it's okay. Stop trying to put a square peg in a round hole. If you aren't meant to be married, stay single and use that free time and energy to glorify God to the best of your ability through the gift (or gifts) He's blessed you with.

Food for thought.

Have a blessed week.

Week 17

"'Lord, if it's you,' Peter replied, 'tell me to come to on the water.' 'Come,' he said. Then Peter got down out of the boat, walked on the water, and came toward Jesus. But when he saw the wind, he was afraid and, beginning to sink, cried out, 'Lord, save me!' Immediately, Jesus reached out his hand and caught him. 'You of little faith,' he said, 'why did you doubt?'" ~ *Matthew 14:28-31*

Fear is probably the biggest killer of dreams because it brings up that question. What is that question? The question of "What if."

A few situations I found myself in a lot were: "I want to do this thing, but WHAT IF I fail?" or "WHAT IF I'm not well-received?" or "WHAT IF they take what I'm saying the wrong way and get offended?"

Okay, that last one doesn't bother me as much anymore. My point is that you can't allow that question to rule your choices when it comes to your future or in general.

Les Brown once said, "The graveyard is the richest place on earth because it is here that you will find all the hopes and dreams that were never fulfilled, the books that were never written, the songs that were never sung, the inventions that were never shared, the cures that were never discovered, all because someone was too afraid to take that first step, keep with the problem, or determined to carry out their dream." And truthfully that question of "what if" is a two-edged sword because, "What if you succeed?" or "What if those words you're scared to say are the very words that are needed to set someone free from whatever it is they're struggling with?" or "What if you offend God by choosing to be afraid of how man will react to what you have to say instead of fearing of what He will do?"

This is food for thought.

Have a blessed week.

Week 18

"Do nothing out of selfish ambition or vain conceit. Rather, in humility value others above yourselves, for not looking to your own interests but each of you to the interests of the others." ~ Philippians 2:3-4

What is selfishness? In layman's terms, it's self-centeredness.

C.S. Lewis said, "Selfishness has never been admired," and William E. Gladstone said, "Selfishness is the greatest curse of the human race." But what does God have to say about being selfish?

God says we should live humbly (by no means does that mean as believers we should be people's doormat).

One could say being selfish is a form of self-worship, in the same way pride is. Be careful and be wary about being selfish, because God opposes the proud (James 4:6). Besides, it's more fulfilling to help other people rather than only yourself, because it pleases God, and at the end of the day, isn't that what we want?

Have a blessed week.

Week 19

"Do not have other gods besides me. Do not make an idol for yourself, whether in the shape of anything in the heavens above or in the earth below or in the water under the earth. Do not worship to them, and do not serve them; for I, the Lord your God, am a jealous God punishing the children for their father iniquity, to the third and fourth generations of those who hate me." ~ Exodus 20:3-8

What is an idol?

An idol is anything that has an excessive hold on your attention and thoughts, and diverts it away from your Heavenly Father.

When people think of idols, they think of statues or some image people bow down to. Such primitive ideology can't exist now in modern times, right?

Let's break down Exodus 20:3: "Do not have other gods besides me." What He's saying here is don't have other gods in His presence (since He's omnipresent that effectively means He's everywhere at all times.)

What can be considered an idol?

Statues and images are prime examples, yes, but there's more to it than that. Anything can be considered an idol if left unchecked, that includes people. A reason why we tend to do that (create idols) is because there's a void we want to be filled But listen, you play a dangerous game placing something in God's place, because God won't play second fiddle to anyone or anything, nor should He have to.

Have a blessed week.

Week 20

"He who finds a wife finds what is good and receives favor from the Lord." ~
Proverbs 18:22

I was talking to one of my cousins once (now, she wasn't a Christian for details I won't disclose), but long story short, she saw the Bible as a book that is degrading to women, because of what it says in the book of Ephesians (Wives submit yourselves to your husbands, as you do the Lord.). This is why it's important to read the Bible for yourself, because she heard this from a second-hand source who neglected to tell her that it also says, "Husbands love your wives, make her holy, to love her as Christ loved the church, give yourself up for her as He did the church, and not to be harsh with them." The New Testament of the Bible is a beautiful love story that speaks on so many levels that not even modern-day literature can hold a candle to. However, people manipulate these passages and scriptures to fit their lives and that needs to stop.

Don't change these words, let them change you.

Have a blessed week.

Week 21

"His wife said to him, 'Are you still maintaining your integrity? Curse God and die!'" ~ Job 2:9

Do you know the devil is a liar? He will always try to get you to doubt yourself or your trust in God. In Job's case, he lost everything but still could endure through faith in God. Don't misunderstand; Job reached a point where he asked God why (Job 7:20). I want to take a moment to say it was a good thing he had a voice of reason in Bilbad the Shuhite (Job 8) at that moment, because that is not a healthy state of mind to be in. At this point, Job was stripped of his children, his health, his wealth, cattle and servants, his own wife whispered sweet nothings in his ear, and he even cursed the day of his birth. Yet, despite all these things that happened to him, he never cursed God. Why? Maybe it was because he knew the power of God and feared him, maybe he knew God wasn't the one to blame for his calamity, maybe it was both or neither. I don't know. What I do know is that this couldn't have been Job's first rodeo, because faith is like a muscle—you have to use it or you lose it, so to speak.

I'm sure some people would probably roll their eyes at the mention of enduring through faith, but unless you've ever been at those low points emotionally where you would curse your name and ask God why He's allowing this, and even wish for your own demise, I don't think you could ever really understand.

Do you know Jesus? 'Cause, if you know him, like really know him, you'll understand that, yeah, life sucks, but at least no matter how alone you may feel at least you have someone in the trenches with you, enduring it with you, and helping you through it.

Have a blessed week.

Week 22

Do not be afraid or discouraged, for the LORD is the one who goes before you. He will be with you; He will neither fail you nor forsake you." ~ *Deuteronomy 31:8*

Life here on earth can be difficult and discouraging at times. During our darkest moments, God offers us courage and strength, if we turn our hearts and our prayers to Him. As believers, we have every reason to live courageously. After all, the ultimate battle has already been won when Jesus died. But sometimes, to live courageously, it's easier said than done, and we become filled with doubts and fears. The answer to our fears is to have faith in God.

The next time you feel yourself being tested, remember you're not alone. Jesus is there with you, every step of the way, so confess your feelings to Him because if you can't be honest with Jesus, who can you be honest with? Man? Man will fail you every time. Tell me I'm wrong.

Call upon God. He's close to the brokenhearted and comforts those who mourn whatever it is that's troubling you. Jesus has your back, but you have to confess, "give up the ghost" in a sense.

Have a blessed week.

Week 23

"And [the Pharisees] asked him, saying 'Why then do you baptize if you are not the Christ, nor Elijah, nor the Prophet?' John answered them saying, 'I baptize with water, but there stands One among you whom you do not know. It is He who, coming after me, is preferred before me, whose sandal strap I am not worthy to unloose.'" ~ John 1:25-27

John, evangelist to many, bold to others, and unashamed until the end. He knew the people needed a Savior and that Jesus was coming.

How devoted are you to Christ? The weight of the cross is not an easy thing to bear. In parts of the world, people die as a result of and for this message, this living water. But take heart, men and women of Christ, there is good news, for to suffer for Christ's sake is a good thing. "Blessed are those who are persecuted for the sake of righteousness, for theirs is the Kingdom of Heaven." (Matthew 5:10)

Never be ashamed or afraid to speak or share the Word of God, because you have no idea whose life you could be saving, whether emotionally or spiritually.

Have a blessed week.

Week 24

"When a Samaritan woman came to draw water, Jesus said to her, 'Will you give me a drink?' (His disciples had gone into the town to buy food.) The Samaritan woman said to him, 'You are a Jew and I am a Samaritan woman. How can you ask me for a drink?' (For Jews do not associate with Samaritans.) ~ John 4:7-9

Why did Jesus and his disciples go through Samaria? During the days of Jesus, Samaria (Palestine) was the capital of the northern kingdom of Israel. Jesus and his disciples were on their way to Galilee from Judea. To get to Galilee from Judea, you have one of two options. Option one is you go around Samaria (like most of the Jewish people did at this time), or you had to go through it.

Now, the relationship between Jews and Samaritans were (and still are) strained because of a birthright that dates back centuries to the days of Ishmael and Isaac, but that's for another time.

Back on topic, why did Jesus go through Samaria? One reason I think was to prove a point. What was that point? He doesn't care who you are, where you're from, what your past was, or the color of your skin.

"For God so loved the world that He gave his one and only Son, that whoever believes in Him shall not perish but have eternal life." (John 3:16)

Actions speak louder than words, and this moment is one of many Jesus would use to challenge people's way of thinking, but also to say, "To hell with the social biases that tear people apart. I came for the Jew and Gentile alike and will unify them both under the mighty hand of the Heavenly Father and will use them to spread the good news."

All it takes is a pebble to create a ripple.

I challenge you this week to reach across the aisle and be the bridge that'll unite people for God's glory. It doesn't take much; something as simple as a compliment can change someone's outlook on not only you but others like you.

Have a blessed week.

Week 25

"The workmanship of your timbrels and pipes was prepared for you on the day you were created." ~ Ezekiel 28:13

These were words used to describe Satan during the time he was called Lucifer. Timbrels or, as they are known in modern times, tambourines, and pipes were built into his very being. He knows how to use music. The intention behind this message is not to strike fear into you; it's said to make you cautious.

"The devil prowls around like a roaring lion looking for someone to devour." (1 Peter 5:8)

Music is a powerful tool. It has the power to bring joy and praise, or it can bring up a slew of emotions you never knew you had and amplifies them. Keep in mind what you take into your eyes and ears.

What or who are you listening to?

Does it come from your Heavenly Father? If not, THROW IT OUT, turn your back on it, and flee. DO not go back to it.

Prayer:

My prayer is that God grants you wisdom and discernment to know what is and isn't from Him, and once you learn, that He gives you the courage and strength to break free. Amen.

Have a blessed week.

Week 26

"The next day, John saw Jesus coming towards him and said, 'Look, the Lamb of God, who takes away the sin of the world! This is the one I meant when I said, "A man who comes after me has surpassed me because he was before me." I myself did not know him, but the reason I came baptizing with water was that he might be revealed in Israel.'" ~ John 1:29-31

John was doing what he was supposed to do: baptizing people in water then encouraging them to repent and informing the masses the time is nigh, for the Kingdom of God was here.

What are you called to do as you wait for Jesus to return? Everyone's answer to this question will be different (if you could do what I could do, and I could do what you can do, one of us is irrelevant). How do you find it? Spending time with the Heavenly Father is a good place to start. By doing so you learn not only more about Him and His nature but you also learn about yourself.

Have you ever been told, "The Bible is not just a book you read, but it's also a book that reads you?" There's truth to that.

What are your hobbies? What makes you feel alive? Follow your instincts and trust in Jesus. The road might be rocky, but once you discover what God's called you to do, nothing can nor will be able to stop you.

Have a blessed week.

Week 27

"And Benaiah, the son of Jehoiada, the son of a valiant man of Kabzeel, who had done mighty deeds, he slew the two sons of Ariel of Moab: he went down also and slew a lion in the midst of a pit in time of snow." ~ 2 Samuel 23:20

Despite only appearing in less than half a chapter in the Bible, Benaiah truly made his mark.

Have you ever heard of a lion chaser? Not a lion TAMER; a lion CHASER. Scripture doesn't tell us what he was doing or where he was, we don't even know his state of mind, but what we see are his actions.

Some fun facts about lions: THEY'RE STRONGER, FASTER and, in most scenarios, DEADLIER THAN THE AVERAGE HUMAN! They can run up to fifty miles per hour and leap as far as thirty-six feet (Needless to say, Benaiah wasn't skipping leg day). Yet, despite all these truths, Benaiah did what most people (give or take Samson) wouldn't even think about doing.

"Thou shalt tread upon the lion and adder: the young lion and dragon shalt trample underfoot." (Psalms 91:13)

My point is that lion chasers, like Benaiah, are cut from a different cloth (Like believers. Read 1 Peter 2:9 for proof). They see an issue, ground themselves, and tackle the problem. Where some people see danger and run, these chasers see opportunity.

Benaiah's actions landed him in the presence of King David. Benaiah wasn't just chasing a lion, he was chasing his destiny.

What are you chasing? Are you chasing things that are drawing you closer to the person God has called you to be, or are you just chasing your tail going nowhere?

Have a blessed week.

Week 28

"But to you who are willing to listen, I say, love your enemies! Do good to those who hate you. Bless those who curse you. Pray for those who hurt you."
~ Luke 6:27-28

Is this an easy verse to follow? No, not by any means. Even though, as Christians, we're supposed to be forgiving and love one another as Christ forgives and loves us, it's not an easy thing to do. It takes a special kind of person to have a Christ-like level of forgiveness.

You're going to have people in your life who hate you whether it's because of the color of your skin, you don't fit society's mold of how you "should" behave, or even because of what you believe. But if we treat our enemies as Jesus described, we become more Christ-like, and living that life is the best life.

"You have heard it said. "Love your neighbor and hate your enemy." But I tell you, "Love your enemies and pray for those who persecute you, that you may be children of your Father in heaven. He causes His sun to rise on the evil and the good and sends rain down on the righteous and the unrighteous. If you love those who love you, what reward will you get? Are not even the tax collectors doing that? And if you greet only your own people, what are you doing more than others? Do not even the pagans do that? Be perfect, therefore, as your Heavenly Father is perfect." (Matthew 5:43-48)

Take some time out of your day today to think about someone who wronged you lately or in the past. Pray to God to give you the strength to forgive them (for your sake), and then do so.

Have a blessed week.

Week 29

"Be still before the Lord and wait patiently for him; fret not yourself over the one who prospers in his way, over the man who carries out evil devices! Refrain from anger, and forsake wrath! Fret not yourself; it tends only to evil. For the evildoers shall be cut off, but those who wait for the Lord shall inherit the land." ~ Psalms 37:7-9

Let's look at a moment in Abraham's life when God had promised him and his wife Sarah (or Abram and Sarai as they were called at the time for the possible sticklers out there) a son. Abraham was eighty-six when he received this news, and it didn't help that his wife Sarah was barren. Now, Isaac wouldn't be born for another fourteen years. Fourteen years is a LOOONG time to wait, especially nowadays with everything moving a hundred miles per hour with no signs of slowing down.

Ever hear the saying, "Good things come to those who wait?" Can you imagine the world we would be living in if Sarah didn't offer her servant Hagar to her husband? I'm in no way criticizing their actions. Far be it for me to do so. I'm only trying to get across that when we're desperate, we do stupid things. In Abraham's case, he was old and that clock was ticking, so in their (Abraham and Sarah's) moment of desperation, they took matters into their own hands, which caused a chain reaction that can be seen to this day with Isaac's and Ishmael's descendants.

The things we do can have tremendous ramifications for our lives, the lives of those around us and, depending on the situation, those who come after us. Don't miss the mark; be patient and wait upon the Lord with fear and trembling. Be obedient and resist the temptation to do things your way.

Have a blessed week.

"Even when I walk through the darkest valley, I will not be afraid, for you are close beside me. Your rod and your staff protect and comfort me." ~ Psalms 23:4

First, God's willingness to provide protection and comfort when we're afraid means God is near and aware. God isn't some distant, disconnected being, as seen as in deism; nor is He nonexistent, as seen through the thoughts of atheists. God knows what you're going through.

Second, God's willingness to provide, protect, and comfort you in times of hardships is a sign that He does care and loves you ... loved you enough to give His only son's life for you.

The verse described fear as a valley, which means we're not always in it, but it is a part of life we all have to go through from time to time. There is nothing hidden from your Heavenly Father, so be honest with Him, share your fears, and trust in Him to protect and comfort you.

Have a blessed week.

Week 31

"Keep your life free from love of money, and be content with what you have, for He has said, 'I will never leave you nor forsake you.'" ~ Hebrews 13:5

I will never leave you ... nor forsake you ... Isn't there so much comfort, so much security in those words? Those eight words have picked me up more times than I can count. Through the pain ... the desertion ... the loneliness ... it's blissful to hear or to read as much now as it was going through those moments. Is God good? Yes, He is. His love is sustaining. How He persists to never let us go, ready to embrace us when we know good (and, well, we don't deserve it), and how He's there to pick up the pieces of your soul what was shattered by others and or our actions, and He does it willingly and wholeheartedly. Why? Because He loves us.

Have a blessed week.

Week 32

"Do not be anxious about anything, but in everything by prayer and supplication with thanksgiving let your requests be made known to God. And the peace of God, which surpasses all understanding will guard your hearts and your minds in Christ Jesus." ~ Philippians 4:6-7

Isn't it crazy how one moment life can be going well, with few issues, but nothing you think you can't handle, and then *BAM!* life comes at you like a wrecking ball, plowing through, shattering your reality (whether it be for good or bad)? Then, the next thing you know, you're in a place you never thought you would be (again whether good or bad)?

But, we as believers should know that, no matter how rocky the waves get, we serve a Savior who can calm those water (if He can, then why doesn't He?) I don't know exactly, but I have two opinions that I don't know if whether or not they are true, and I'm not going to be the one to flip that coin to declare them to be fact. I'll still put them on the table and let you decide:

Opinion #1: He lets us go through certain things (whether by our own stupid choices or just by "chance") to humble us and teach us a lesson.

Opinion #2: He allows it to happen so that today's tragedy can be tomorrow's testimony.

Who knows? Maybe I'm talking crazy talk. Nonetheless, my opinions aside, when calamity strikes, we as believers have to know where our strengths lie.

Do you know where your strength lies? It lies in Christ, in prayer, and trusting in the Lord, knowing that He has good intentions for us and won't let the devil destroy us.

Can the devil hurt us? Sure (for one reason or another), but never destroy us. Look no further than the life of Job to see that. Trust in the Lord that He has your back, and when life comes, know you have someone in your corner who's closer than a brother.

Have a blessed week.

Week 33

"And he arose and came to his father. But while he was still a long way off, his father saw him and felt compassion, and ran and embraced him and kissed him." ~ Luke 15:20

The prodigal son squandered his inheritance, spent it on useless things, lived in the here and now, (much like Esau now that I think about it), but when he came to his senses, it was too late, that money well had dried up, those who he had thought was close to him in that season were gone, and he was eating with the pigs. So, what did he do? He decided to go back to his father's home, and on the way, he rehearsed what he would say when he saw him again. But, to his surprise, his father ran out to meet him, embraced him, and kissed him. Isn't that the perfect picture of us and God when we screw up? We do something ignorant, or turn our back on God and choose something over Him, thinking that thing (whatever it may be) will fulfill our needs and find out that's not the case, and then hopefully fall on our knees to repent, and beg that the Heavenly Father would forgive us and not rain down fiery justice upon us. Instead, we're met with not anger, but an embrace, and Him saying, "My child who was lost is now found. Let's rejoice!"

If there's anything to be taken away from this week's message, it's this: God's not mad at us. He loves us, If anything, He's madly in love with us.

Have a blessed week.

Week 34

"And without faith, it is impossible to please God, because anyone who comes to Him must believe that He exists and rewards those who earnestly seek Him ... By faith, Abraham, when called to go to a place he would later receive as his inheritance, obeyed and went, even though he did not know where he was going." ~ Hebrews 11:6, 8

Can you imagine how hard it must have been for Abraham to leave his family to go to a place unknown, an instruction given to him by God, whom his family didn't even know, but Abraham trusted Him enough to leave them and venture into the unknown?

Ever heard of the saying, *"Talk is cheap?"* It's one thing to say you're going to do something and planning it versus actually doing it. And through faith, Abraham did it. He left his parents, his traditions, and his family, except for his wife and nephew, and departed to a place only God knew he was going to.

It's scary to take that first step. It's also the hardest. But, once you take that first step, the next one is easier, and the next one becomes easier than that one, and so on. If God tells you to go do it, He might just be leading you to your "promised land."

Have a blessed week.

Week 35

"By faith, Abraham, when he was tested, offered up Isaac, and he who had received the promises offered up his only begotten son, of whom it was said, 'In Isaac, your seed shall be called,' concluding that God was able to raise him up, even from the dead, from which he also received him in a figurative sense." ~ Hebrews 11:17-19

Do you trust God with the things He blessed you with? If you do, good job; you're ahead of the curve. But if you don't, why? All things belong to Him (Psalm 24:1) and if He created it, that means He understands how it operates. Or do you have so little faith in our Heavenly Father that He doesn't know what He's doing?

Abraham knew God was faithful, and no matter what, he could trust God. Don't believe me? How many of you would sacrifice your child to God? A good parent would say, "Are you insane? Heck no!" but a wise one would say, "Though I may not want to do this, Lord, I trust You. I trust Your ways are higher than mine."

Isaac was the child of promise (Gen. 18). God told Abraham that his descendants would be as the stars in the sky (Gen. 15:5). God is many things, but a liar is not one of them. Do you think Abraham doubted when God told him to sacrifice his son? Probably, he was still a parent. I can imagine his heart racing as he was about to do the deed, but in the end, he was willing to do what God asked of him.

Are we that obedient? How far does our obedience go, as far as it benefits us or as far as God wants? Abraham passed his test, will we pass ours? Remember, God never goes back on His word.

Have a blessed week.

Week 36

"And David spoke to the men who stood by him, saying, 'What shall be done to the man who killeth this Philistine and taketh away the reproach from Israel? For who is this uncircumcised Philistine, that he should defy the armies of the living God?'" ~ 1 Samuel 17:26

Whose authority are you under? Are you under the Lord's mighty hand of protection? If yes, then why are we running when He's called us to take ground? When He's told us to be strong and courageous? (Joshua 1:9) Fear? Don't fear God is with us. He strengthens, helps, and upholds us with His righteous right hand. (Isaiah 41:10) Condemnation? There's no condemnation for those in Christ Jesus. (Romans 8:1) The devil? Resist him, and he'll flee. (James 4:7) Can you command the devil? A true follower of Christ can.

When Jesus called the Twelve together, he gave them power and authority to drive out all demons and to cure diseases. (Luke 9:1)

We need to stop playing church and realize that being a follower of Christ isn't a game, it isn't a Sunday thing to post a #LOLIAMHUMBLE. The world is hurting, and we know the Doctor, but some of us just sit on the sidelines and watch as the world devours itself. Why? You don't have to do something big and bombastic to make an impact in this world, to make it better. Something as simple as a compliment, giving a smile, offering to pay a part of someone's groceries ... PAY FOR THE GROCERIES. Remember going into this week that giving of yourself pleases the Lord.

Have a blessed week.

Week 37

"But you are a chosen people, a royal priesthood, a holy nation, God's special possession, that you may declare the praises of him who called you out of darkness into his wonderful light." ~ 1 Peter 2:9

Do you believe you're worthless? Well, if you do, think again. Everyone is here on purpose, which, by proxy, means you have worth. Granted, what your purpose is, I can't tell you. That's between you and the Lord. Pray to Him and ask for a revelation.

I remember when I went to Victory Christian, they had a creed: "I am here on purpose because I have a purpose ..." I've kept those words close to my heart, and they were along with some other choice sayings that got me through some bleak times.

Whenever you feel like giving up or just stop altogether, remember one of two things: one, that you're not here on accident, you have a purpose; and two, your life is not yours to take (and here's a bonus: You are loved).

Have a blessed week.

Week 38

"Now, when the turn came for Esther, the daughter of Abihail, the uncle of Mordecai, who had taken her as his daughter, to go the king, she requested nothing but what Hegai, the king's eunuch, the custodian of the women, advised. And Esther obtained favor in the sight of all who saw her." ~ Esther 2:15

It's important to have a wise council. In Esther's case, her council came from Hegai, and his words would have determined the fate of her and her nation (Israel). Thankfully, she followed his instruction to the letter.

Wise leaders listen and learn from others (George Washington is another example of a leader who was good at heeding instructions from others).

Who's in your council? Where are they leading you? Is it closer to your calling, or are they driving it away?

Have a blessed week.

Week 39

"Anyone who meets a testing challenge head-on and manages to stick it out is mighty fortunate. For such persons, loyally in love with God, the reward is life and more life." ~ James 1:12

Going through trying times can be difficult, but there's a light at the end of the tunnel, and when you look behind, you'll see the grace and mercy God used to carry you through it and rejoice. Don't give up; endure. Pressure makes diamonds, and what a beautiful gem you'll be when it's all said and done. I know it looks disastrous right now, but look at it this way: no mess, no message.

Have a blessed week.

Week 40

"Brothers, if anyone is caught in any transgression, you who are spiritual should restore him in a spirit of gentleness. Keep watch on yourself, lest you too be tempted." ~ Galatians 6:1

First, let's look at what transgression is. The dictionary describes transgression as "an act that goes against a law, rule, or code of conduct; an offense." So, what is Paul saying here? If a believer is doing something that goes against God's laws, you should stop them. He's saying, the body of Christ should look after one another, to hold each other accountable, and if one of us is led astray, correct them, and not out of anger or condemnation, but out of love and compassion. He also cautions us to guard ourselves, because if we're not careful, we might get ensnared, along with the person we're trying to protect.

Be cautious, be wise, and look after one another.

Have a blessed week.

Week 41

"As for me, this mystery has been revealed to me, not because I have greater wisdom than anyone else alive, but so that Your Majesty may know the interpretation and that you may understand what went through your mind." ~ Daniel 2:30

Do you know that everything you have comes from God, ranging from your health to your position at work? There's no power that doesn't come from God. (Romans 13:1). Translation: you're in that position at work because God allowed you to be there. This even extends to what He allows us to know (this isn't a word on gratitude, but now would be a good time to give the Lord some praise).

Humility is the name of the game this week. God loves a humble person. Now, that doesn't necessarily mean He wants us to live in squalor, but to have a humble heart.

What does a humble heart look like? One name: Jesus. Selfless, valuing others above yourself, being a servant, realizing that this life isn't about you, that it's about Him (Jesus), and the things He's done, is doing, and will do. Where does one learn to be humble? Start with surrendering yourself to Jesus.

Have a blessed week.

Week 42

"Do you not know that, in a race, all the runners run, but only one gets the prize? Run in such a way as to get the prize." ~ 1 Corinthians 9:24

Dreams are extremely fragile in the beginning, during their developmental stages. Imagine planting a (insert your favorite vegetable here) seed in the ground and only leaving it in the ground and watering it for a day then uprooting it. Did you or anyone get anything from that? A rumbling stomach maybe, but not what you were envisioning. Now, take that same seed, put it in the ground, care for it, water it, prune it, and whatever else needed for that seed to thrive, and see how that, now you have what you were aiming for, now you can feed yourself and others. That's how dreams operate.

If your dream's a God dream, then your dream's not just going to benefit you. It'll benefit others, as well. That's how it worked with Joseph. But be careful, because new dreams are fragile. Give them time to grow.

Now, this part is important: don't tell anyone about your dream. I know this goes against the grain of what society teaches us, but listen to me, because nothing will kill that dream faster than someone else's opinion. Trust God to let you know when it's time to let others in on what you're goals and dreams are.

Have a blessed week.

Week 43

"So how do we fit what we know of Abraham, our first father in the faith, into this new way of looking at things? If Abraham, by what he did for God, got God to approve him, he could certainly have taken credit for it. But the story we're given is a God-story, not an Abraham-story. What we read in Scripture is, 'Abraham entered into what God was doing for him, and that was the turning point. He trusted God to set him right instead of trying to be right on his own.'" ~ Romans 4:3

We spend a lot of time waiting on God, waiting on Him to move, to make some sort of miracle. But, what if the reason you're not getting your breakthrough is because God is waiting for you to move? Are you being obedient to the Holy Spirit? Maybe the reason you haven't received your breakthrough is because you're not heading where you're supposed to be going? Maybe God's waiting for you to meet Him at the place He's called you to go? God is always moving, working, preparing all on our behalf, but we have to do our part, whatever that may entail (listen and trust the Spirit).

Have a blessed week.

Week 44

"For a just man falleth seven times, and riseth up again: but the wicked shall fall into mischief." ~ Proverbs24:16

I read a quote once by Tom Bodett that rang true to me. The quote said, "In school, you're taught a lesson, and then given a test. In life, you're given a test that teaches you a lesson."

Though we may get knocked down, we can't afford to stay down. As a matter of fact, while you're down there, devise a way to prevent getting knocked down again. That way, when round two comes around, and it will, you'll be ready.

Have a blessed week.

Week 45

"Do you not know that if you present yourselves to anyone as obedient slaves, you are slaves of the one whom you obey, either of sin, which leads to death, or of obedience, with leads to righteousness." ~ Romans 6:16

What Paul is saying here is that we become slaves of what or whomever we continue to obey. Who are you listening to? The small voice you know to be God or the roars of the crowd? Obeying God, though not easy, leads to righteousness and blessings (might be disguised) granted to the path there is, jagged most of the time, but the alternative is sin, which leads to death and ruin. Granted, it may not seem like it at first, yet slowly but surely, it'll destroy you and affect those around you. So, be wise and watchful.

Have a blessed week.

Week 46

"The heart of man plans his way, but the Lord establishes his steps." ~ Proverbs 16:9

Do we know how to rest in God's sovereignty? Well, living outside of His sovereignty is prideful. When you're working outside His authority isn't that like saying, "I don't need Your authority because I know what's best for me?" That is pride, which God opposes.

How do we rest in God's sovereignty, though? Well, one way that comes to mind is he'll make us. (Psalms 23:2) Another way is a bit more tricky, given the world we live in today. Now, follow me on this. ...

Stop ... Disconnect ... Tune out the hustle and bustle of the outside world and relax.

When was the last time you mellowed out? "My schedule doesn't allow me to *mellow out.*"

I remember when I was in high school, my history teacher had an abbreviation for a word. That word was B.U.S.Y., which meant *Buried, Under, Satan's, Yoke.* Our bodies aren't designed to be running on all cylinders all the time. That's a surefire way to be miserable and loathe yours and everyone's existence. That's not to say to be lazy, either. You gotta know your limits and find a balance.

I'm saying this because, by resting, you can reflect and see His power, reflect on the struggles He brought you out of, see where His grace saved you when your enemy had you dead to rights, the doors He opened that you didn't even know to knock on. Resting in God's authority means you trust Him and not lean into your own understanding.

Take this week to honor the Sabbath. Take a rest and reflect on how God has been.

Have a blessed week.

Week 47

"You will have plenty to eat, until you are full, and you will praise the name of the LORD your God, who has worked wonders for you; never again will my people be shamed." ~ Joel 2:26

Do you know who your provider is? Hopefully, you know it's the Lord God Almighty, Jehovah Jireh. "The Lord will provide." He's always there, behind the scenes, making a way for His people and meeting their needs.

Jesus said, "Look at the birds of the air, for they neither sow nor reap nor gather into barns; yet your heavenly Father feeds them. Are you not of more value than they?" (Matthew 6: 26). Personally, I'd like to think I'm a bit more valuable than a pigeon.

As we sit around the table with our families this week, let's give God praise for allowing us to see another year, another chance to give Him thanks for all that He's done, the plots of man He foiled, the protection He's provided, and the love He's freely given to us.

Have a blessed week.

Week 48

"And he withdrew himself into the wilderness, and prayed." ~ Luke 5:16

What does your one-on-one time with your Creator look like? Do you have one-on-one time with your maker? It wouldn't hurt to begin one. In fact, you'll only benefit from having one.

Taking time to meditate is important in a believer's life, and you can pretty much do it anywhere. You don't necessarily have to be at home; you can do it in your car or wherever else you have a moment alone.

How do we expect to learn the Lord's voice if we don't take the time to slow down and listen for it?

If I said it once, I'll say it again: we can't always be firing on all cylinders, which I hate to say is a major problem in this country. We're constantly moving, constantly "striving." Never taking a moment to take that step back and reflect, to relax, to see the goodness of the Lord to appreciate what He's done for us. But that's a side note (an important one, though). God's always talking, but if you don't stop, you'll miss what He's saying.

I'm not judging anyone, because I'm guilty of it, too.

How should our one-on-one time with God look like? Well, I can't answer that, because for one, everyone's personal relationship with God is different. But praise and worship is as good a place to start as any. Let the Holy Spirit guide you and go from there. It could lead you to a variety of places, like the Word of God, to scripture you never thought to read, or maybe it'll leave you in a state of praise. It's not always the same, which is a fun way how God likes to operate.

Have a blessed week.

Week 49

"Know this, my beloved brothers: let every person be quick to hear, slow to speak, slow to anger; for the anger of man does not produce the righteousness of God." ~ James 1:19-20

It's really easy to give in to anger. At the same time, anger has its purpose, just like sadness, happiness, and love have theirs. Some benefits to anger are: it motivates us to solve problems, it projects our true feelings toward certain issues, and it's ironically quite calming (depending on who you vent to). But, for every positive, there's also a negative.

Anger, if left unchecked, could mess up our life. Marriages have ended because a spouse couldn't keep their temper in check, and people are in jail because they let their anger persuade them to make a choice that they'll regret for the rest of their lives. So, in short, yes, it's normal to get angry. It happens to the best of us. If it can happen to Jesus, it'll happen to you. But don't dive headfirst into anger. You, and most certainly those around you, might not like the results.

Have a blessed week.

Week 50

"So, because you are lukewarm, neither hot nor cold, I am about to spit you out of my mouth." ~ Revelations 3:16

Jesus called the church in Laodicea "lukewarm." Back in those times, it wasn't good to drink things that were lukewarm. To do so was seen as distasteful (it was also because they tended to harbor diseases, but that's how Jesus felt about the church there—distasteful.

It's better to be either hot or cold for Christ rather than in the middle of the road. Why? What's so wrong with being "lukewarm?" If you're "hot," you know Christ; if you're "cold," you don't know Christ (though you still have a chance to know Him). People who are "lukewarm," they know just enough about Jesus to get by, they're easily swayed, they don't want to know Jesus on a deeper level, they show little enthusiasm when it comes to the things of God, and they have a difficult time when it comes to hearing God's voice. And as God's word says, "He'll spit them out of his mouth."

I hope you choose to be "hot" for God, not just this week, but all the days of your life.

Have a blessed week.

Week 51

"Therefore the Lord Himself will give you a sign: The virgin will conceive and give birth to a son, and will call him Immanuel." ~ Isaiah 7:14

Immanuel means "God with us." Isn't that assuring? Through our highs and our lows, on our sickest and our healthiest days, no matter where we are in life, He's there, toughing it out with us. You are never alone.

The holidays are the roughest time, financially, for people, just to "keep up with the Jones," so to speak, or to meet family expectations, and that's not the point of Christmas at all.

Christmas isn't about material things, like all these corporations would like you to believe. It's about the birth of our Savior, Jesus Christ, the one who sticks closer than a brother, and the Son of the living God. And we should never lose sight of that.

As we celebrate this week the birth of our Savior, let us remember all the things He's brought us out of, the dreams He's given us, the expectations met, and the miracles He's performed this year and all of the ones He'll do for us from next year.

Have a blessed week.

Week 52

"This Book of the Law shall not depart from your mouth, but you shall meditate on it day and night, so that you may be careful to do according to all that is written in it. For then you will make your way prosperous, and then you will have good success." ~ Joshua 1:8

Quick question: how can you know God's character, let alone His voice, if you don't spend time in His presence? In short, you don't. You can't just show up to that building on Sundays and expect that to be enough. I'm not saying you have to run down to the building every Sunday, because there can be some wicked people in the building. What I'm saying is, if you want to know God, you have to get in His word and make it a part of your life, and when you learn and understand His word, you'll gain a deeper understanding of His love for His creation (i.e. You), among other things.

His word also equips us for the spiritual battles we'll inevitably face. Lastly, His word also teaches us how to live our lives and not in a GET BACK IN LINE MIND SLAVE kind of way, but more like a cause and effect sort of way. There's a whole book dedicated to just that. It's called Proverbs.

Plus, getting to know God is necessary for faith-building. If you don't know Him, how can you trust Him, or do you go around trusting strangers?

Okay, so do we study God's word? Read it, meditate on it, practice it. I mentioned Proverbs; let's look at Proverbs 9:8: "Do not reprove a scoffer, or he will hate you; reprove a wise man, and he'll love you." Study this scripture, meditate on it, and see how you can use it in your day-to-day life.

Have a blessed week and Happy New Year!